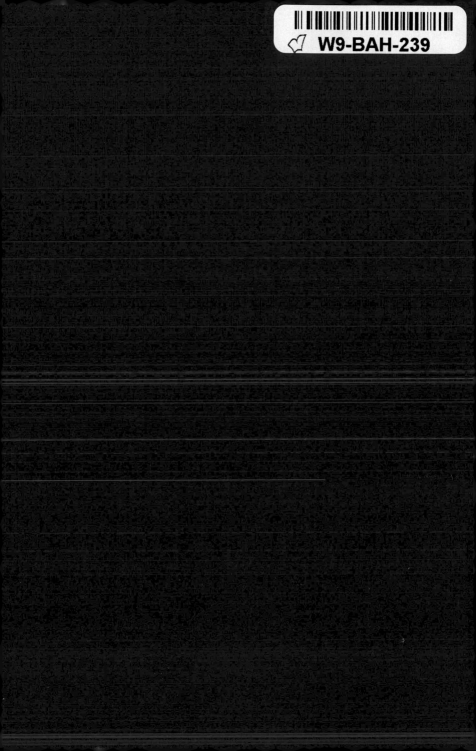

TESTAMENT

POETRY
A Scottish Assembly
Sharawaggi (with W. N. Herbert)
Talkies
Masculinity
Spirit Machines
The Tip of My Tongue
Selected Poems
Apollos of the North
Full Volume
Simonides

ANTHOLOGIES
Other Tongues: Young Scottish Poets in
English, Scots and Gaelic (editor)
The Penguin Book of Poetry from Britain and Ireland
since 1945 (editor with Simon Armitage)
The New Penguin Book of Scottish Verse (editor with Mick Imlah)
Scottish Religious Poetry (editor with Meg Bateman and James
McGonigal)
The Book of St Andrews (editor)

NON-FICTION
The Savage and the City in the Work of T. S. Eliot
Devolving English Literature
Identifying Poets: Self and Territory in Twentieth-Century Poetry
The Modern Poet
Scotland's Books: The Penguin History of Scottish Literature
Robert Burns and Cultural Authority (editor)
The Scottish Invention of English Literature (editor)
Heaven-Taught Fergusson (editor)
Contemporary Poetry and Contemporary Science (editor)
The Bard: Robert Burns, A Biography
Bannockburns

TESTAMENT

Robert Crawford

CAPE POETRY

Published by Jonathan Cape 2014

2 4 6 8 10 9 7 5 3 1

First published in Great Britain in 2014 by
Jonathan Cape
Random House, 20 Vauxhall Bridge Road,
London SW1V 2SA

www.randomhouse.co.uk

Addresses for companies within The Random House Group Limited can be found at:
www.randomhouse.co.uk/offices.htm

The Random House Group Limited Reg. No. 954009

Some of these poems first appeared in *Edinburgh Review*, *Headshook* (Hachette), *London Review of Books*, *Mimic Octopus*, National Trust for Scotland, *New Poems, Chiefly in the Scottish Dialect* (Polygon), *Scottish Literary Review*.

A CIP catalogue record for this book is available from the British Library

ISBN 9780224098076

The Random House Group Limited supports the Forest Stewardship Council® (FSC®),
the leading international forest-certification organisation. Our books carrying the FSC
label are printed on FSC®-certified paper. FSC is the only forest-certification
scheme supported by the leading environmental organisations, including Greenpeace.
Our paper procurement policy can be found at www.randomhouse.co.uk/environment

Typeset by Palimpsest Book Production Ltd,
Falkirk, Stirlingshire

Printed and bound by
CPI Group (UK) Ltd, Croydon CR0 4YY

for Alice, Lewis, and Blyth
with love

If you unlock
What is locked inside you
What is inside you
Will save you,
But if you never unlock
What is inside you,
That is the lack
That will kill.

The Gospel of Thomas, 70

CONTENTS

HARD-WEARING FLOWERS

NIGHTINGALE FLOOR

Odalisque, so pendulous and slim,
As I nibble and lick your oxter,
Glutted with the rush of your curves,
I image us as a nightingale floor,
All perfect plainness, tiny cries
Born from surprise, ecstatic danger,
Dovetailed with joinerwork of love
As we fit together, tongue and groove.

LONGING

Over the standing stones of Machrie Moor
Starlight discharges midges across Arran.
The sea is a heron's breast; desire
Moist lips in front of banked thunderclouds.

Daylight, an orthopaedic surgeon,
Resets the nation's bones,
Realigns the cave of Robert the Bruce
With mobile-phone masts, fingers veins of whin
Shining along the pit bings of Lanarkshire, attuning
Hip-hop to incunabula.

Kissed nipples; water sucked through a straw;
Slow, body-heat pull; stashed pollen
Carried in a shirt, catkin kisses,
As you close your eyes, then open again,
Intimate places tallied and caressed –
Hand-smoothed kegs of butter.

Let the cold British Empire statues
Weigh down our squares. We'll slip
Into start-up now, fields stubbly with orchids,
City streets laceworked with light,
Everything we were threatened with and scared out of

Bright today, wedded to our independence,
The held look, the Luckenbooth brooch.

TREPIDATION

The leaves are leaving the trees, and you will be leaving.
The waves are beating as always on the castle rocks.
This day will pass. I have got it over with,
Said what had to be said, and heard
What I never wanted to hear.
I shall sit, reading Candia McWilliam,
And listening so intently I'll catch,
Miles off, a night train approaching.
I shall listen for you as long as I live,
Listening in sickness, listening in health,
As McWilliam listens, not just around corners,
But to birds' nests woven in hawthorn hedges,
'Right into the egg within the nest.'

BOOKFACE

Yours, Bookface, that rapt, intent look,
Part photographer's, part graphic artist's
Gaze of engrossment, nose in a book,
Body in a book, head over heels,
Zooming to that part of the planet where
In St Andrews, Glasgow, Edinburgh,
Even in the cities of one-child China,
No one is an only child.

YOUR FEET

When you walk out, screaming,
'You're so righteous, so self-righteous!'
I am numb.

I want to speak to you as Neruda
Addressed the woman he loved,
Calling her 'little leaf', 'little bird',

But I love you just because you'd scorn
These phoney diminutives. I want
To write a poem in praise of your feet,

Slim, elegant, librarianly, nimble —
Your crossed right sometimes dangling a shoe —
And how they have walked you to me now.

HARD-WEARING FLOWERS

I love you because you love Harris tweed,
How it's several times slumped into bankruptcy,
Business plans hauled back from the dead,
Only to find itself again
Slyly prized, mixed with moorlands
Honeymooners have mooned on, sheep
Trotted deftly across. I love you
Because you hug its sparkle and dourness,
Dyed-in-the-wool strength, sphagnum-moss green, peaty reds.
To wear tweed is to put on the planet,
Checked or unchecked, islands, hard seas, air threads
Woven from the world's greatest democracy,
The disunited states of Harris.
I love you more than the Golden Road
(So called for the cost it cost to lay)
To the south, to Rodel, a tweed route great
As the silk roads of Marco Polo;
And now, when flood-tides of haute couture
Sweep in on catwalks, new-wave fashionistas
Mocking thrawn fruits of the looms
Of Tarbert or Luskentyre,
I love you because even here tonight,
Among matt, arty party jackets
And smart-assed, drab bankers' suits
You still say you love Harris tweed.

PERSIAN

I long to catch you at Waverley Station.
I see you with my eyes shut tight.

★

As soon as I enter a crowded room
I know you are there. I steel myself
Against rushing to stand at your nape.

★

From the *Bustan* of Sa'di: *I woke one night,*
So alert I could hear a moth
Whisper to a candle, 'I am your lover.
Burn me. Why are you crying?'

Till the candle replied, 'Love is not for you.
Fire scares you. I have to stand erect
Till I melt to zero. I may scorch your wings,
My own flame consumes me head to foot.'

A LITTLE HISTORY

DECLARATION

My name is Scotland. I am an alcoholic.
Sexism runs through me as through a stick of rock.
For all my blotchy pinkness, I am determined
To be less prim about my gene-pool, more airily cosmopolitan;
To love my inner Mary, my Floral Clock and John Thou
                              Shalt Knox.
I can live fine without nuclear subs.
I've built far too many warships.
All I want now is my dignity back,
To stand on my own unsteady feet,
Sobered up, but not too sober, to renew
My auld alliance with this tipsy planet,
My dependence
And my independence.

BURNSWEAR

Welcome, Fifth Minister. Thank you for rushing
To open Robert Burns's World of Shoes.
Thirteenth of fourteen global Burnswear Centres,
We are the showcase for the Bard's old boots,
Pumps, cootikins, and miscellaneous footwear.
Fifth Minister, we're proud that we brought home
To Scotland for the Year of Homecoming
Those kick-ass metal toecaps that The Bard
Had shipped ahead to Ayr Mount in Jamaica
Where he once thought to do some work with slaves.
We have his well-licked boots. We boast a slipper
Slipped from the slim left foot of Highland Mary.
Professors may pooh-pooh their provenance,
But these wee stilettos of the Mauchline Belles
Rival the buffed-up, scuffed heels of Dumfries,
Clarinda's lace-ups, and yon nineteen socks
Burns never wore but kindly autographed;
Daddy Auld's lost galosh; Ann Park's neat latchets;
A front right cast by Tam o' Shanter's mare;
And best of all The Bard's own dancing shoes
In which he reeled and set and crossed and cleekit.
Fifth Minister, your own discovery
Of twenty thousand lost poems by Burns
Stashed in his left Nith wader sets us first
Among the cultural industries. Nintendo
Wii Sleekit Cow'rin Tim'rous Beastie kickers
Mark a strategic, world-class Scots renaissance
In Burnswear, and I hope that here today
Before going back to your constituency
You'll try a pair of Standard Habbie Brogues
Inlaid with toadying crowns and union jacks
(Said to be favoured by Sir Kenneth Calman),
Available in Old Fettesian

Blair Black or British Skint Kirkcaldy Brown.
See how they fit your feet, Fifth Minister.
They come gift-wrapped, your own parcel of brogues.

POLE DANCE

Flapping unflaggingly in the brisk wind,
Sub specie aeternitatis,
Saltire spun from the words 'almost there',
Proud flag of our neverendum.

DAVEHEART

St George o' Osborne tae his richt
And SamCam by his side,
Daveheart has ridden thro' the nicht
Tae flatter Scotland's pride.

He sing the joys o' Union lang
And loud through shitty weather.
His een are bricht. His voice is strang,
'We're better aff thegither!'

O Daveheart, man, bewaur the wiles
O slippery Smart Alex
Whose henchfolk mibbe seem aa smiles
But sound like Gaelic Daleks.

Aw Daveheart, will ye muster men
At Cumnock or Port Seton?
Nae every battle's won, ye ken,
On the playin fields o Eton.

The Paps o Jura are yir ain,
Though nae the chaps o Govan.
The faithfu, met in Bearsden's rain,
Look awfie like a coven.

Daveheart, your michty sword aloft
Shines like a nuclear weapon,
But as ye gang by coo an croft
Tak tent o whit ye step on.

'Welcome tae Scotland!' as is said
By yon auld guy in *Skyfall*.
Our Leader's thrawn, an' overfed.
Our scenery's an eyeful.

17

For aa the Cabinets ye've chaired,
Trust neither man nor wumman.
We arenae scared. We're just prepared.
The Camerons are coming.

FLODDEN

Flooded with blood, sodden, splodged
Second Agincourt for England,
The Scots king just one of those flowers of the forest
A' wede awa at yon blood-red midwives'
Breech-birth of the British Empire.

BEACH MUSIC

in memory of Bill Millin

The victory is not gained by the men at arms, who manage the pike and the sword; but by the trumpeters, drummers, and musicians of the army.

David Hume, *A Treatise of Human Nature*

Mad lad,
Lone
Piper,
That was one
Crazy chanter-blast
As the D-Day troops
Stumbled past,
Cut down round you
When you shouldered your drones,
Dressed to kill
In your father's kilt,
Proud
Like Fingal
In a Gaelic song,
As you showed
Under loud
Long
Heavy fire
In the mire
Of Normandy
How David Hume
Was right,
That at the height
Of battle
Victory is not gained
By men with bren guns

Or through the rattle
Of stens,
But by a pale,
Shit-scared musician
Who stands and plays
Like hell at the heart of the hail.

MARCH PAST

First up tiptoe a bunch o wankers
Wi placards, 'GOD SAVE SCOTTISH BANKERS'
Aw whit a big parade
Johann leads aa the unemployed,
A wee bit pinched and underjoyed
Aw whit a big parade
Proud Edward Milibrand and Sir Ming
Join arms tae dance a Hielan Fling
Aw whit a big parade
The polis mak a great co-ordon,
'Och, let me in!' cries Zombie Gordon
Aw whit a big parade
And next as far as een can see
Special Advisers check IT
Aw whit a big parade
The woofers woof, the mikes aa screech,
Big Alex blatters oot his speech
Aw whit a big parade
Wee Ruthie croons, wi mony an oath,
The Declaration o Arbroath
Aw whit a big parade
Pairched STV and BBC
Slink aff wi Nicola for tea
Aw whit a big parade
Frae Jenners, Harvey Nicks, and Thrums
There's gamelans and pipes and drums
Aw whit a big parade
Kids chant frae Duns tae Aiberdeen,
'We've got the vote at sweet sixteen!'
Aw whit a big parade
A monumental line o floats
Revs up: 'Noo, gie us aa yir votes!'
Aw whit a big parade
Ma frien says, 'Let's get hame at last!

We've seen the end o' yon March Past,'
Aw whit a big parade
But then dark-suited, tiptoein men
Come roun the corner aince again. . .
Aw whit a big parade

THE BANNOCKBURN COMPASS

Northward strong mountains
Stand sentinel under rain.
You can trust their gneiss.

★

Under equal skies,
Friend, embrace this weathered place,
Ready for what comes.

★

Eastward at daybreak
Larks sing, and sharp light reveals
Who it is you kiss.

★

For as long as one
Hundred of us can still stand
We fight for freedom.

★

Southward the vineyards
Ripen, hot empires wrestle,
Geese vee overhead.

★

You will need good friends,
Mither, faither, dochter, son,
When the crisis starts.

★

Westward at sunset,
Friskily under eyelids
New dreams are circling.

★

With this ring I wed
Dog heather, Scots thistles, hope,
The Bannockburn wink.

IN MEMORY OF DONALD DEWAR AND ENRIC MIRALLES, ARCHITECTS OF THE SCOTTISH PARLIAMENT

Standing-stone-thin man, though you have fallen,
You marked our path beneath the Merry Dancers,

And Scotland found the measure of your name
Between mirage and miracle, Miralles.

THE SCOTTISH CONSTITUTION

It must contain silver sands. It must hold water
In the shape of lochans, hydro dams, and firths.

It must be just, in the sense both of perjink
And even-handed, shaking hands with all.

It must be old, with the wisdom of the rookie,
It needs to know its onions, has to laugh

And dance at weddings, all recriminations,
Selkie stories, fiscal memoranda.

It must be shy, tongue-tied, then eloquent,
Catching your eye and holding it forever,

However far you go, to whatever shores,
Atolls or cities, it must hold you fast.

REVEILLE

Wake up, new nation,
Stretch yourself. It's time
To fling the covers back, and sing,
Alarm-clock loud, a sharpened trill of song
Greeting the daylight now that dawn has broken,
You who have slept so long – too long –
With one eye open.

GREIK

eftir Cavafy

WAAS

Wi nae obleegement, nae peety, nae a sklent o shame,
They've biggit waas aroun me, strang an heich.

An noo I hunker here, wanhope chittlin ma wame.
I cannae sei past this weird. I'm dune. I'm dreich.

I'd sae sae muckle tae be daein still, ootby.
Aa yon days they biggit the waas, hoo come I didnae ken –
    it's daft –

But I nivver heared yon biggars, nae ae saft soun, but gey
Certie, bit by bit, they've snibbed me aff.

Walls

With no kindness, no pity, not a sideways glance of shame, they have built walls around me, strong and high. And now I crouch down here, despair nibbling my heart. I cannot see past this disaster. I'm exhausted. I'm dreary. I had so much still to get on with, out there. All those days when they built the walls, how come I did not realise – it's stupid – but I never heard those builders, not one soft sound, though absolutely surely, bit by bit, they have cut me off.

PITTIN UP A WURD

A sailor drooned oot i the Minch.
Anawaurs, his mither gangs an lichts
A lang, skrank caunle afore Oor Leddy's ikon,
Pittin up a wurd he'll sune be hame, an the wedder lown –
Her lug aye hearkenin tae the wund.
Whill she hunkirs an pits up a wurd,
Yon ikon taks tent, sairious, dowie,
Kennin the laddie she bides for'll nivver be hame.

*A sailor drowned out at sea. Unaware, his mother goes and lights a
long, slender candle in front of Our Lady's ikon, praying he will soon
be home, and the weather fair – her ear all the time attending to the
wind. While she crouches and prays, that ikon pays attention, solemn,
sad, knowing that the boy she waits for will never be home.*

KIRK

I luve the Kirk: its session hoose,
communion plate, communion taibil,
the auld manse, the glebe, the pulpit.
Whan I gang intae a Scots kirk
wi its bare wuid pews,
its metrical psalms,
the skinklin blak brogues o the meenisters
gaunt in their corbies' goons,
the pechin Doric warsle o their prayers –
I aye hink o yon Scots 'wha's like us',
yon heritable glore o John Knox.

*Skinklin – sparkling; corbies' goons – crows' gowns; pechin – deeply
sighing; warsle – wrestling; hink – think; heritable glore – inheritable
glory.*

I couldnae find thaim – tint lik snaa aff a dyke –
The saft een, the peely-wally face in the vennel
At dayligaun. . .

I couldnae find thaim – mine jist by luck –
Sae easy tint
Syne pined for.
Yon saft een, yon peely-wally face,
Yon lips – I jist couldnae find thaim.

Tint lik snaa aff a dyke – lost suddenly like snow off a wall; saft een – soft eyes; peely-wally – pale; vennel – alley; dayligaun – dusk; easy tint – easily lost; syne – then.

THE GOD FORLEETS ANTONY

in memory of Maimie Hamilton

I the howe o the nicht whan suddentlie ye hear
An inveesible parawd stravaigin by
Wi aa its braw muisic, its clack,
Dinnae mane for yir sonse that's misgaein noo,
Wurk gane agley, yir gran ploys
Daith caunles – dinnae mane for thaim yisslesly:
Lik ane lang redded up, an gey wicht,
Say fareweel tae her, tae Embro wha's hastenin awa.
Mind an nae mak a daftie o yirsel, dinnae say
It wis aa a drame, jist a swick o the lugs:
Dinnae bemean yirsel wi tuim howps lik yon.
Lik ane lang redded up, an gey wicht,
As is richt for ye wha wis gied a toon lik this,
Awa stievely tae the winnock
An hearken wi a muckle hert,
But nae wi the girnin an fleetchin o a coof:
Hearken – yir lang an last delicht –
Tae the clack, the braw, braw muisic o yon unco parawd,
An say fareweel tae her, tae the Embro that for ye's gey
   near tint.

The God Abandons Antony

In the depth of the night when suddenly you hear an invisible parade
strolling past with all its beautiful music, its chat, do not lament your
luck that is failing now, work gone wrong, your great plans turned to
supernatural lights that warn of impending death – don't lament for
them uselessly: like someone long prepared and very strong, say fare-
well to her, to Edinburgh that is hurrying away. Remember not to
make a fool of yourself, don't say it was all a dream, just a trick of
the ears: don't demean yourself with empty hopes like those. Like

someone long prepared, and very strong, as is right for you who were given a town like this, away resolutely to the window and listen with a great heart, but not with the complaining and fawning of a fool: listen — your long and final pleasure — to the chat, the lovely, lovely music of that remarkable parade, and say farewell to her, to the Edinburgh that for you is very nearly gone.

HAME

As ye stert for hame
Tak tent o the lang road bak,
Aa mervels, aa whigmaleeries.
Marget Thatcher, Sawney Bean,
Butcher Cumberlan – dinnae fear thaim;
Ye'll nae bump intae trash lik yon
As lang's ye keip a guid, stoot hert,
As lang's a really guid carfuffle
Fires ye up boadie an sowl;
Marget Thatcher, Sawney Bean,
Butcher Cumberlan – ye'll ne'er meet thaim
If ye dinnae cairt thaim alang in yir ain sowl,
If yir sowl disnae caa thaim tae greit ye.
Tak tent an tak the lang road bak,
Lat ther be monie simmer morns whan, simply leuchin,
Ye set in herbours nivver seen afore;
Set in at ootlandish free ports whaur
Ye get guid gear:
Queer curale, lammer, ibone,
As monie, monie parfumes as ye can;
An visit, tae, a wheen o ootlan ceeties
Tae lear lik bejants in their ootlan college.

Aye keep yir hame in mind, hame's whit ye're for.
But dinnae hurry, mind an tak yir time
Sae that ye're trauchled by the time ye're bak,
Gey auld an bien wi aa ye've tuik aboard,
An nae expeckin hame tae mak ye bien.

It wis yir hame that gied ye this lang road.
Wi'oot hame, ken, ye'd ne'er hae stertit oot.
An noo yir hame hes naethin left tae gie ye.

Stert — start; tak tent o — pay attention to; whigmaleeries — fantastic contrivances; carfuffle — excitement; leuchin — laughing; curale — coral; lammer — amber; ibone — ebony; a wheen o ootlan ceeties — many foreign cities; bejants — first-year students; mind — remember; trauchled — exhausted; bien — prosperous; gey auld an bien — very old and prosperous; gied — gave; ken — know.

THE MARBLE QUARRY

THE MARBLE QUARRY

For the second time in fifty years
I come to the Marble Quarry.
Last time, a boy, I came with my father.
Now I am here with my son.
Afternoon heat streams from the marble,
White light chipped from the earth.
At the quarry's hoist and jetty
Underwater abandoned altars,
Veined slabs, shine through the waves.
We eye up shards among the scarred,
Discarded blocks. I tell my son
How my dad handed me a monumental
Offcut, heavy as an unfinished temple.
We scour what's left. I pick a piece
That fits my hand, and hand it to him
Gingerly. It fits his hand too.

GUIDE

Year in, year out,
The guide still follows
A well-paced route
Through those small rooms
Until the tour-group
Have all been told
And told again
About the diarist,
About the poet,
Brother and sister,
Husband and wife;
So their plain life
Stays still
Green in the rain,
The stress
Less on fame
Than on wee mundane
Details:
How He once failed
To neatly ink His name
Inside the lid
Of His sole suitcase,
Though He did
Just
Find space
For that last aitch
North of the rest
Of WORDSWORT
And hunched in the small
Window seats
You can hear
Repeated
Still
Year in, year out,

How they strode off-road
Down gills, by crags,
Over the hills,
Then nightly cleaned their teeth
With salted twigs
Dipped
In polishing soot
From the grate, the hearth,
And how The Great
Poet of the Heart
Walked and talked
And talked and talked
About his cuckoo clock;
How Mrs De Quincey tripped
With a bucket of coals;
How Coleridge called
Then later screamed,
Locked
In an upstairs room's
Opium dream;
How when winter came
They skated on the lake,
William nicely
Getting his skates on
To slice
His zigzag initials
Precisely
As he whizzed
By on the ice;
How, through long nights,
They quizzed
Friends,
Lighting a candle's rush-light
At both ends;
How, fond of good food
At his Edinburgh club,

Walter Scott thought
They downed too much porridge,
So sneaked out a window
To dine well at the pub;
How every five weeks
They washed their underclothes;
What the rent cost;
How frost
Made the children ill
And how those children slept
Cold, and no doubt wept
In their room upstairs
Above the downstairs chill
Of an underground stream
That streamed
More and more
Up through the floor
Of that slate-floored larder;
How Mary
Loved Point d'Angleterre lace;
And the whole place,
Dark now, was dark then,
Walls all smoke-blackened, reeking.
Think how
Year on year
At Grasmere
Each trained guide's voice
Goes on speaking
These shining trivia
In one
Unbroken
Spoken
Song;
Until,
Before long,
Another

Voice starts
To master the art,
Comes to take over
The guiding,
Learning in order
Through just walking round:
The wash-stand's lesson,
The step's confession,
Each teacup's balance,
Each lintel's silence,
Each hinge of sound.

SITHS

Studious condensed clouds, thin,
Pliant, oily; or corn-fed,
Pecking grain like black crows,
They are congealed air, living in clefts.
You see on high hills'
Tillage the prints of their furrows.
They echo and outlive us
With strong, moist ointments,
Slim, honed weapons of flint.
Cut in two, they reunite like rain.
Flitting, with unextinguishable lamps,
Busy and silent, their agile clans
Pass us by night. We wake, remembering
The sullen, cold stroke of their hands.

RAGWORT

after the Gaelic of the Carmina Gadelica

Remarried, he keeps seeing his first wife rise
From her grave and rush in to kiss their children,
Then stare hard into his second wife's eyes
And scold her for the way she pulls ragwort.

HERAKLEITOS

eftir Kallimachos

Herakleitos,
Whan they telt me
Ye'd deed
Wey bak,
I grat,
Mindin
Yon nicht
We sat oot gabbing
Till the cauld
Peep o day.
An sae, ma auld
Halikarnassian pal,
Ye got seik
And noo ye're someplace
Deid in the grun –
But thae sangs, aa
Yon nichtingales o yourn,
Still soun
Lik they sounded
Then
When we set oot
An sat oot,
Twa young men.
Daith taks the lot,
They sey,
But, ach,
Thae sangs
He's nivver
Gonnae get.

in memory of Mick Imlah

telt – told; deed – died; grat – wept; gabbing – talking; peep o day
– dawn; seik – ill; grun – ground; yourn – yours; soun – sound.

MICK IMLAH

Than Orpheus befor Pluto sat doune,
And in his handis quhyte his harp can ta . . .
Henryson, 'Orpheus and Eurydice'

The day you died I stared up at the grey
Dome of St Paul's, then caught the sleeper north,
Dourly imagining your own departure
From London as your last, pained way to stay
Elusive, Mick, Oxonian Aberdonian,
Sly Doric fitted up by your posh voice,
Your sports-star, film noir, flaneur's loucheness spooked
By the meth-kissed phantom City of Dreadful Night.
I have your stoic email, a few postcards'
Nibwork. When I think of your dark ink,
What flits back is the sound of a Fife blackbird
Singing the day I first heard you were ill –
One drop-dead Orpheus; though I could not spot it,
And when I tried to, then its song just stopped.

SALUTE

Ewart Alan Mackintosh, 1893–1917

As on the Somme in 1917
You learned to be both one thing and another,

Saxon and Gael, tentative and commanding,
Gentle man, good killer, gentleman,

So I salute your poet's guilt, the fact
Of not knowing who it is a man salutes.

SHADOW

Is it a sign of sprightliness or age
When my shadow now reminds me of my son's?

TESTAMENT

THREAD

My faith
Hangs by a thread.
It always has.
No point
Spending long
Going over it,
Worrying,
Will it snap?
Will it go?
Is it the wrong
Kind of faith?
Better just to take it
And sew.

JOHN THE BAPTIST

While you were gabbing at the water cooler
Lovingly I poured a vial of water
Into the gubbins of your computer

So when you came back that gasp of surprise
As you stared with disbelieving eyes
Was the shock of one newly baptised.

STARS

Told,
Foretold,
They rode
Through untold
Bone-cold nights,
Dismounting
To be counted
In the old
Heartland
Of the clan,
Where, shacked up
Some way
Through their stay
On a flight
Between wars,
True to type
His stubborn
Fiancée
Gave birth
On trampled earth
Under the stars
To a lad
She lagged
Like a pipe
And stashed scratchily away
In a hay
Bed
Made
From a big tub,
A bin
In a shed,
Where the kiddie cried
Not far
From where they'd tried

But failed
To get in
At the hoaching pub.

Luke, 2: 3–7

CATCH

After day
After day
Walking
By the lochside,
Watching
Two men
Trying
To cast their net,
He said,
'Forget that.
Here's the way
People
Catch
People.'

Matthew, 4: 18–19

LOCH

Storm-tossed
As they rowed
Across
At night
Against the wind
They found
He nearly passed
Right
By,
Striding
On the loch,
Till they cried
Out
With a wild shout
And he said,
'Och,
Don't worry,
It's me,'
Then strode
Aboard
As the storm
Stopped,
The wind dropped,
And silently
They held their breath,
Scared to death,
Laughing.

Mark, 6: 48–51

WRITER

When the young married woman
Who slept around
Was brought to him,
He wrote on the ground
With his finger.
Then
The men
Said,
'Our law demands
She be stoned.'
He went on
Writing on the ground
As if
In the middle of a poem.
They lingered,
Nagging him,
'What do you say?'
Till he lifted
Himself to full height
And spoke:
'Hey,
I want one of you
Clever
Men
Who has never
Sinned
To chuck the first rock.'
Then
He began
To write
Again
On the ground
Until one by one
They started to walk

Away,
So he and the woman
Were left alone.
He spoke: 'Lass,
The oldest
Man
Went first,
The youngest
Last.
I think now
Today
Justice is done.'
She saw how
It was just as
He said.
No
Accuser remained,
And she heard him add,
'Go.
If you sinned
Before,
Sin no more.'

John, 8: 3–11

TOTAL

He saw the rich
Slip costly gifts
Into a box
And saw too
A widow
Drop in two
Small
Pennies.
'So,'
He said,
'I tell you,
This poor
Widow
Put in more
Than all
The rest,
For they
Offered their many
Gifts
As small
Change,
But she,
Though so poor,
Gave her all.'

Luke, 21: 2–4

Squaddies
Lugged him inside
Their desert base,
Yelled
To their mates,
Chucked a purple
Coat over him,
Stuck
A bramble crown
On his head,
Saluting,
'God save the fucking King
Of the Jews!'
Three crews
Beat him red
With a stick.
Spat sick at him,
Knelt down
In the sand,
Bowed,
And,
When they had done,
Taunting him,
Tore off
The purple coat,
Shoved him
Coughing
Into his own clothes,
Dragged him out
Over the hard
Length of the yard

Then hoisted their bloody King
All the way up
His tall cross.

Mark, 15: 16–20

MOP

Noon. The sky
Turned dark.
The moon
Burned black
Till three o'clock.
He gave a cry:
'*Eloi,*
Eloi,
Lema sabachthani!' –
'O
God,
O
God,
Why
Have you let me go?'
Some,
Listening, said,
'Hear that?
He's crying
For Elijah.'
One
Ran up
With a sponge
On the end of a stick
Like a sick
Mop,
Held it up,
Vinegary,
To sop
His lips,
Taunting,
'Hey!
Let's see
If Elijah

Will be
His saviour now!'
Then with a hoarse
Cry
The teacher died.
The curtain
Of the temple
Tore
Floor
To ceiling,
And a soldier
Of the occupying force,
Posted there
In front of the cross,
Said,
'All along
This man
Was God's Son.'

Mark, 15: 33–39

'If I don't see
The mark of the nails
In your palms;
If I can't jam
My fingers in the holes
Made in your hands,
Then for me
There can be
No faith.
To understand
The truth
I must
Stand
And thrust
My hand
Into the wound
In your side.'
So Christ said,
'Clutch
What was the dead
Flesh of my hand,
Touch
My red,
Split side
So the truth
Can no longer
Be denied.'
Then Thomas, stronger
For hearing that,
Did

What he said
And said,
'O my God.'

John, 20: 25–28